THIRTEEN AND GROWING

Thirteen and Growing
Copyright © 2023 by Debora Ann Cole Dockett

Published in the United States of America

Library of Congress Control Number: 2024900963

ISBN   Paperback: 979-8-89091-461-3
ISBN   eBook: 979-8-89091-462-0

All rights reserved. No part of this publication may be reproduced, stored in a retrieval system or transmitted in any way by any means, electronic, mechanical, photocopy, recording or otherwise without the prior permission of the author except as provided by USA copyright law.

The opinions expressed by the author are not necessarily those of ReadersMagnet, LLC.

ReadersMagnet, LLC
10620 Treena Street, Suite 230 | San Diego, California, 92131 USA
1.619. 354. 2643 | www.readersmagnet.com

Book design copyright © 2023 by ReadersMagnet, LLC. All rights reserved.

Cover design by Tifanny Curaza
Interior design by Don De Guzman

THIRTEEN AND GROWING

TO STEAL OR NOT TO STEAL

UNACCEPTED FRIENDSHIP

YOUR TRASH IS MY TREASURE

Debora Ann Cole Dockett

TO STEAL OR NOT TO STEAL

Thomas Carr was very angry with his father this morning. Before leaving for school, he didn't get his allowance. He neglected to clean the yard as he should have the day before.

Everybody was going to a basketball game between the boys in class 8-1 and the men teachers. Now, of all days, he didn't have money to buy a ticket.

"Dad, please! I'll...."

"No, Thomas! You should have done as I asked you yesterday!"

"But Dad, I'll miss the game and everyone is going!"

"Sorry, son. You should have thought about that before you goofed up; now get going before you miss your bus!"

When Mr. Carr turned his back, Thomas threw up a clenched fist, slammed the door, and immediately regretted what he'd done because his father humiliated him further by making him come back to reclose it correctly.

When he reached the bus stop, everybody was chattering excitedly about the event.

"I hope Mr. Cox doesn't have a heart attack," laughed one boy.

"Ha! Are you kidding?! The man jogs five miles a day, and that's before we get to school!!!"

When Thomas joined the group, he angrily flopped his books down on the sidewalk.

DEBORA ANN COLE DOCKETT

"Man! You look like someone just put ice in your shorts!" said Eric.

"Yeah," said Greg. "What's wrong with you?"

"Everything! My Dad woke up grouchy this morning."

"Your Dad? He's usually a nice guy!"

"Not this morning!" said Thomas. "He would not give my allowance!"

"You? Broke?! Now that's a laugh," snorted Daniel.

"No it's not. Now I can't go to the game!!"

"Aw man! I feel sorry for you!" exclaimed Pete.

"If you had come a few minutes earlier, I could have loaned it to you, but my sister asked to borrow it," said Dennis, "Now I'm broke."

"Same here," said Mike.

"Rats!" said Thomas as he kicked a rock.

When they reached school, talk was everywhere about the upcoming game! Boys, girls, teachers, everyone! He became more upset and anxious. His English teacher, Mrs. Moore, was a kindly older woman who sometimes forgot things. This morning (of all times), when she placed her purse in a chair next to her desk, she forgot to close it, and Thomas spied a five-dollar bill sticking halfway out.

"Man, I could use that!" he thought to himself.

He sat there and debated with himself as to whether he should take it or not.

THIRTEEN AND GROWING

"She's a nice lady," he thought. "But I could use the money.... Nah! I shouldn't take it. She helps me out a lot...But I would pay her back.... It wouldn't actually be stealing."

Suddenly he heard his name being called.

"Thomas, would you please come back to the class with the rest of us!!"

Teetering, snickers, and giggles could be heard all over the classroom.

"Huh? Oh...I-I'm sorry."

He was afraid that someone may have seen him staring at the open purse. The game and five dollars were heavy on his mind. Thomas was a whiz in English, but today he made a D- on a test. When the bell rang, Mrs. Moore, as all teachers, would stand at the door, waiting for students as they came and left.

Thomas was the last one to leave the class. As he passed Mrs. Moore's desk, he quickly picked the five-dollar bill from her purse. At first he almost hesitated, but he really wanted to go to the game. Throughout the next class, he could not study. Now that money wasn't the problem-- guilt was-- "Why did I do that? I shouldn't have !!" he thought.

"I could have asked her to let me borrow it, but people would think I'm a nut if I asked to borrow money from a teacher.

"It was now one- thirty. The game was scheduled for 3:00.

"If I give it back, I'll be in trouble and if I keep it, everybody will be in trouble."

He fidgeted all through the next class. Something kept saying to him, "Give it back! Give it back!"

Guilt was losing out to the sweet thought of that exciting game that was only one and a half hours away. Again, his train of thought was interrupted by the thundering voice of his science teacher, Mr.Storm.

"Carr!" he growled. "Can you answer my question!"

"Question? What question? Oh...No... Uh...n-no Sir, I can't."

"Do you even know what the question was?"

"What question?"

"Carr, are you alright?

Still half in thought, he answered,

"Yes, I stole it."

The entire class howled with laughter.

"Stole what, Carr?" asked Mr. Storm.

"Sir?!" he asked in alarm. "Did I say stole? I-I meant told....yeah.... yeah, that's what I meant. Told."

Mr. Storm just stared in confusion.

"Carr, do you need to see the nurse?"

"No, Sir! No, Sir! I'm fine. I promise I am."

"Well, you better straighten up and pay attention!"

When the bell rang at two-thirty, Thomas' heart began to pound.

THIRTEEN AND GROWING

"Thirty minutes before the game!" he thought.

He imagined that the bleachers would be full and how everyone would be screaming and going wild. This is going to be some volleyball game! He made up his mind! "Bleachers, here I come."

He wiggled and squirmed in his seat until the bell sounded. The last class would be cut by 30 minutes. Anxiety was killing him. At the sound of the bell, kids nearly trampled one another to get to the gym. Being in that noisy, pushy line was one of the best things that could happen to him. At least, that's what he thought at first. He overheard one of the students say something about how poor Mrs. Moore said she had to skip lunch because she had misplaced some money. That did it!! He tore out of that line, hating himself for doing such a dumb thing. Just before he reached her room, he said to himself,

"Anything she does to me, I deserve it."

When he stepped into her room and saw her beaming smile, he hated himself even more.

"Hello, young man, what can I do for you?"

"Well...I... Uh....Would you...."

"Yes?"

"I don....'t know how to...."

He just shoved his hand into his pocket and took out the five-dollar bill and hung his head as he handed it over to Mrs. Moore.

"What's this?"

"Your money," he replied.

"My mo..... Thomas Carr! You didn't!"

"Yes, Ma'am, I did, but I am very, very, very sorry and I know that I deserve whatever happens."

"But why, Thomas?"

He paused, then he spoke.

"I wanted to go to the game really bad and my father wouldn't give me any money because I didn't do what I was supposed to...but I was going to do it today once I got home." "Never put off today for tomorrow! As you can see, that did not work out...did it? Why didn't you just ask me?"

"I thought it was dumb to borrow money from a teacher," he said.

"No, it is not dumb. You wouldn't be in the situation you're in now
if you had asked."

"I am so sorry and I will never do it again."

"Tell you what, this time you will get off with 2 weeks of detention. But you must never ever do this again!"

"I promise I won't!!"
She nodded and shooed him out.

He had never been so troubled and guilty in all his life.

"It's not worth the torment," he thought, "I don't see how Crooks can be crooks! My conscience would bother me too bad." And he never took anything again that didn't belong to him.

THIRTEEN AND GROWING

UNACCEPTED FRIENDSHIP

Today would be the first day of public school for Darren Skyhawk.

Ever since he could remember, he and his family had lived on a reservation in Missouri. Now, they were moving into the city and even before he knew anyone, he knew he would not like it.

As he made his way into the classroom, he resented being stared at. The unfriendly faces were scowled with prejudice and hatred...something he had heard about but had never had personal experience. He was suspicious of everyone and trusted no one. He became even more withdrawn when kids called him Geronimo, or told him to do a rain dance which made kids laugh.

Kevin King was in his first period class. He hated it when the class jerks would tease and make fun of Darren if the teacher stepped out of class for a moment.

"Hey everybody," yelled David. "Big-Chief-Stuck-Up, got no tongue. Cat got it!"

Everybody became quiet, wondering what was coming next.

"Hey Gee-ronimo, how 'bout some rain, boy!"
Darren never uttered a word. Some of the students laughed; others didn't. Kevin was one of those who didn't. Thomas and Jim danced around in circles, whooping and hollering as David ambled over to sit beside Darren,

"Say...uh...Gee-ronimo, where's you make up? You must not be a for real Indian cause you ain't got no feathers."

"David, why don't you just leave the guy alone!" demanded Kevin. David turned around and glared at Kevin.

"Who asked you, Mr. Four-Eyes?!" sneered David. Thomas and Jim came and stood at both sides of Kevin's desk with folded arms as they foolishly sniggled at David's insults. David annoyingly looked at one boy first, then the other, then said, "You guys laugh at his dumb jokes because you're as stupid as he is!"

"You act like you like him or something!" said David.

"Probably does," said Jim. "They're both weird."

Kevin was getting fed up with these bullies. He stood up to Jim as he pushed his glassed back on his nose.

"What if I do?"

Jim was surprised to see Kevin stand up to him. He was also about two inches taller. When the teacher stepped back through the door, everyone went back to their seats as they hissed threats at each other. Darren was glad that he didn't have any other classes with those goof-balls. His father warned him that something may happen but to try to stay peaceful. He didn't expect it to happen so soon though. At the end of the day, he met Kevin at the end of the hallway.

"Hey, Darren," he said, "how are you getting home?"

"My Mom's coming to pick me up. Want a ride?"

THIRTEEN AND GROWING

"No."

"What's wrong with you?' I'm just trying to be your friend!"

"Don't need friends," said Darren as he walked away. Suddenly, he stopped walking.

"Hey!"

Kevin walked back to meet him.

"What's up?"

"Don't stand up for me. I can fight."

"S-sure.... W-whatever you say."

Darren walked a few steps as Kevin looked on, then slowly turned and bowed his head in gratitude. As he started to continue home, David and his friends showed up.

"Hey, boy," said David. "We don't like the way you look."

"Yeah, we've got enough problems with other misfits, so we decided we don't need no add-ins to our problems, understand, boy?"

"Your problem," stated Darren.

"Uh-uh, Gee-ronimo," said Thomas. "Your problem!"
Kevin watched in the distance as the action began. They all Threw their books to the ground. A couple of them took their shirts off and rolled up their sleeves.

"Never mind, guys!" said David. "He's all mine!"
Before David knew what had hit him, Darren had kicked him so hard in his mouth that the only thing he could do was to scream

out in pain. The other boys looked at one another and backed away in fear and disbelief at what they had just witnessed.

"Who's next?" asked Darren. "I'm ready."

Nobody answered. Darren casually walked over to Thomas and Jim. Walking right up to their faces, practically nose to nose, he said,

"If either of you bother me again, you will be sorry. If you have something to say to me, say now or say never!!"

Thomas and Jim were almost too afraid to breathe.

"I go now," stated Darren.
When he left, the others walked over to see if David was okay.

"Wow!" said Jim. "I'm going to make sure that I never have to deal with him."

"You guys was supposed to have my back! Where were you chickens?

"When I saw that guy lift his leg, spin around in the air, and kick you like that, I said uh-uh, I can't take that chance!"

"What are you going to do now, David?" asked Thomas.

"Go to the principal's office first thing in the morning and make up a lot of junk so that Punk will get kicked out of school."

The three boys laughed at the joke as they went on their way.

Kevin had never left the scene, and he was glad that he had not. Upon hearing the mean plan that Kevin was cooking up, he decided he would go home and call the principal and explain everything to him. When he looked around, Darren had disappeared out of sight.

"He is a fast mover in more ways than one," thought Kevin.

He turned and trotted towards his home. Once he reached home, he called Mr. Scott.

"Hello?"

"Is this Mr. Scott?"

"Yes?"

"This is Kevin King."

"Ah! Kevin! What can I do for you?"

"I was calling about something that happened this afternoon at school."

"Go on."

"Do you remember Darren Skyhawk?"

"Our Native American student? Yes, I remember him."

"There are three guys in my class who bully him."

"Uh-huh," Mr. Scott answered thoughtfully.

"Their names are David Joneston, Jim Ruthnig, and Thomas Thomas."

"Oh, those three. I've had problems with those boys for Quite some time now.... go on."

"Anyway, Sir, they started a fight with Darren today and they were going to come to your office in the morning with a fake story. I saw the whole fight."

"Alright, Kevin. I appreciate your telling me. Darren is Already withdrawn from everyone and I'm glad you are in his corner. By the way, did anyone get hurt?"

"Well, Darren kicked David in the chin and busted his lip, but that was all."

"Thank you, Kevin. I appreciate the information."

"You're welcome."

"I hope Darren can see that I'm only trying to help. I hate to see bullies picking on others."

The next day, Kevin could not believe what his eyes were seeing when he saw David. He had a large patch over his chin and had what he figured was red food dye smeared all over the patch.

"Man! You look terrible!" exclaimed Jim.

"You mean grotesque!" laughed Thomas.

"Thank you, Gentlemen!" said David.
The three guys were bursting at the seams.

"If you guys think this is funny, wait till you hear my sad, sad story," said David as he made a sad pouty face. Again, the guys howled with laughter.

Suddenly Thomas spotted Kevin. He hunched David and Jim. Kevin saw David's lips form "watch this." They didn't notice That Kevin had been observing them.

"Hey, Kevin, see what your friend Geronimo did to me? The boy is a savage! I can't believe you're always defending him!"

"Maybe if you guys would leave him alone, you wouldn't have

THIRTEEN AND GROWING

To worry about getting beat up."

"I can't believe you! He tries to kill me and you're still on his side!" Kevin only shook his head and walked away. When they reached the school, Darren was standing in his usual place. When he saw David, his expression remained unchanged.

"What are you staring at, Geronimo?"

"Pale-face ghost."

"We'll see who's the pale-face ghost when I come from the office.

"I'll go to office with you. You will lie."

When they reached the office, Mr. Scott was sitting at his desk in his office. The secretary told them to go in.

"May I help you, Gentlemen?"

"Mr. Scott, this boy has been causing a lot of trouble since he's been here at our school."
"Oh? What kind of trouble, Joneston?" he asked as he pulled his glasses from his face.

"Well, Sir, he's been picking fights with people and he knows that they can't beat him up because he knows some kind of martial arts.

As a matter of fact, I thought I'd better come to you right away!!"

"Really now?"

"Yes, Sir. I know you probably noticed this bandage on my chin."

"Plainly," he stated in an unconcerned way.

"He caused this!"

"He? Who is he?" asked Mr. Scott in a sarcastic voice. David pointed at Darren.

"That boy over there." Then he gave an unconvincing wince.

"Ow!!! It hurts when I talk!!!!"

"Oh really?" asked Mr. Scott. "Let me have a look."

"No!" David said as he grabbed his face and stepped back.

"It hurts too much!"

"Well, you show me."

"Sir?!"

"I want to see your injury…for insurance purposes…you know."

"It may get infected if I uncover it."

"Just for a second. I promise I won't touch it," he said with an unconvincing smile."

David dropped his head with a sigh as he removed the dressing.

"Tsk! Tsk! Tsk!" said Mr. Scott as he shook his head at David.

"Shame on you, David! Why did you do this? Why do you hate Darren so much?"

"Well, because he's different."

A frown came upon Mr. Scott's face.

"Because he's different?!"

THIRTEEN AND GROWING

"Different?! That does not give you or anyone else the right to judge people. How would you feel if people judged you because you had freckles? Or if they teased you because of your way of life?

Have you tried to help him in anyway? Pointed to a class? Walked with or along beside him and held conversations?"

"No," said David as he looked down at the bandages and cotton in his hand that he took from his face.

"I think an apology will be a good starting point," said Mr. Scott.

"Now, shake hands."

David put out his hand to shake Darren's hand and Darren spat in David's hand.

Everyone looked at Darren in surprise. Mr. Scott frowned and grimaced.

"Darren, Why'd you do that? We're trying to make amends so that everyone can go on their way peacefully. Maybe you two could become friends."

"No. May I go now?"

Mr. Scott just scratched and shook his head in defeat.

"Look, guys, this should have never happened!!! For the next five days, I need to see the two of you in my office. We've got personality adjustments to work on. By the way, anyone else who was involved…. You, too."

Then he walked away. The two guys glared at one another,

but no one said a word. When they reached the class, anticipation was on the faces of everyone to hear what happened. David looked at everyone, frowned, and told them to stop being so nosy. Darren went straight to his seat and didn't make eye contact with anyone. When he settled into his desk and class began, Kevin talked to him in a low tone.

"Hey Darren, how did everything go?"

"Fine."

"No trouble?"

"No."

"You cool with everything?"

"Yes."

When Darren looked at Kevin with what seemed to be a look of satisfaction, Kevin felt that the ice was just a little closer to be broken and peace was on the horizon.

YOUR TRASH IS MY TREASURE

Danny! How come every time I take your pants out to wash, I have the feeling that I'm going on a hunting expedition?!"

"What do you mean, Mom?"

Danny's mom pursed her lips together and held her hand out.

"This!"

In her hand was a screw, a round thing with a hole in the middle, a funny-looking rock, a metal clip, and various articles.

"Should I throw these things away?"

"Are you kidding! That's my good stuff!"

"Good for what? Junking up my house?"

"You don't understand, Mom," he said as he took the things from her hands. "I use this stuff for other things."

"Oh yeah?" she asked as sarcastically as she put her hands on her hips.

"Sure! See this clip. I can pretend that it's part of a mountain climbing kit for my toy man."

"If you say so," she sighed.

"And this?"

To her, it looked like the end of a suspender.

"I can pretend that it's part of a crane. And this……"

"Okay!! Okay!! I believe you! Just keep it out of my way."

He smiled at his mother and sprinted through the door. Across from his house was vacant lot and today something had happened. The lot had been cleared. "Oh boy!" he

thought to himself. "Look-a-here, Look-a-here! The lot has

been cleared. That lot has 'come here, Danny' written all over it! I'll bet that it's filled with lots of things that I could use. I've got to go get Billy and Joey."

He leaped from his porch and raced down the street to Billy's

house. When he knocked on the front door, Billy's sister, April, answered.

"What do you want?"

"Is Billy here?"

"What if he is?"

Danny threw up his hands in disgust.

"Look, just go get him! I ain't got time to argue with you! This is important!"

"Maybe it is to you, but it's not to me!"

Billy finally came to the door to see who was there.

"Danny! Scram, April!"

"I don't have to."

Billy gave her a slight shove.

"Go on! Beat it!"

She formed a big pout with her lips and begin a fake sob.

"Im'ma tell Momma on you!!"

"Go ahead! See if I care!"

She ran out, screaming and calling for her mother.

THIRTEEN AND GROWING

"Your sister's gross."

"Yeah, she makes me sick too.... sometimes."

"How do you put up with her?"

"She's my sister…. I have to. Anyway, what's up?"

"You'll never guess what!"

"Tell me. I can hear the change in your voice."

"You know the lot across from my house?"

"Yeah, what about it?"

"It's been cut! So that means…. It means I'd better get thing-a-ma-jig box! Wait for me! I'll be back in a flash!"

He returned about 10 minutes later.

"What took you so long?"

"April had my good junk scattered all over my room and I had to chase her to get some of it! You ought to be happy you don't have a sister."

"I am so happy that I don't have a sister. Let's go get Joey!"

When they opened the gate to Joey's yard, they saw his little brother, Ralphie.

"Oh boy! If you think April is bad…"

"I know, I know! Ralphie is a monster!"

When he saw the boys arriving, he yelled,

"Hey, Joey! Your creepy, dumb jerk-face friends are here!!!!"

"Be quiet, you little creep!!"

"I'd rather be a creep than either one of you!!!"

He took a handful of dirt and threw it at them and ran inside.

Joey looked at the two of them and humped his shoulders.

"Sorry, guys."

Danny looked at Billy and said,

"I'd rather deal with April any day."

"Hi, guys," said Joey.

"What's up?"

"Know that field across from Danny's house?"

"Yeah."

"It's been cut."

"Good! A collector's dream! I know what you're getting at! I'll be right back."

When he went inside, Ralphie stood at the screen door Making faces and licking out his tongue at Joey and Danny. When something diverted his attention, Danny swooped down and grabbed some dirt. Joey saw him and began to giggle. Danny walked up to the door while talking calmly to Ralphie.

"Ralphie, what have we ever done to you?"

"Nothing. I just don't like you."

"If you don't change, other kids won't like you either."

"So what? I won't like them either."

He began to make faces again. Just as he shut his eyes tightly and stuck out his tongue again, Danny jerked open the screen door and slapped the dirt on his tongue. It surprised Ralphie so much that he quickly shut his mouth which didn't stay shut very long. He let out a squeal like a scalded pig.

THIRTEEN AND GROWING

Joey came running out of the house with his things.

"I don't know what you did, but thanks! Let's go before Mom calls me back!" They cut through their neighbor's hedges and made their way to Danny's house.

Their eyes widened when they saw the clean-cut field. To make things even more exciting, Danny had a metal detector.

"Can I use that?" asked Billy.

"Me, too?"

"Sure. After I use it first," bragged Danny.

The three boys looked the field over before starting.

"There's got to be some good stuff out here," said Joey.

"There's no telling what, what, what."

"Calm down Billy! There's enough space out here for all of us."

They started out in different directions. Danny started out first with the metal detector which immediately began to beep loudly, which brought the others running to him.

"I don't know what I found yet. I've got to dig or look under the grass a little way."

Joey and Billy stood silently, but fidgeted, as Danny looked for his treasure. To their surprise, it was an old silver dollar coin.

"When can we use it?"

"I'll use it for a few more minutes, then you guys can use it."

"Me!" demanded Joey.

"No, me!" demanded Billy.

"We'll flip my dollar and whoever gets his call will use it next."

As the coin flipped in the air, Joey called heads and that's how it landed.

"It's settled," said Danny. "Good luck!"

And they all went back to their spaces. After about fifteen more minutes of exploring, Danny called, "Anybody find anything else?"

"Yeah, but let's wait till we finish to show what we have," said Joey.

"Okay."

"Fine with me."

The three boys all went back to their different places and started again. Every now and then they would hear a "Wow" or "Awesome" or "Great." Although there was hardly any conversation between them, they were
having the time of their lives.

Danny's mom had been watching them the whole time and was amazed at how much patience they had! For nearly 4 hours, they looked endlessly for boyish treasures without getting tired. She prepared sandwiches, chips,
and something cool to quench their thirst, and carried it to the picnic table.

"Danny! Joey! Billy!"

The three boys ran over and their eyes immediately spied the refreshments she had prepared.

"I've been watching you boys and I figured you could use a break."

"Yes! Thanks, Mom."

"Thanks Mrs. Nelson!"

"You're the best, Mrs. Nelson!"

THIRTEEN AND GROWING

She smiled and returned inside. Joey's thing-a-ma-jig box was loaded and Danny's pocket was loaded and Danny had found some treasures also.

"You guys will never guess what I found."

"I found some neat stuff, too!"

"Ha! Wait till you see what I have."

The boys munched happily on their snacks and talked about what they had found and what they had to do to get it out of the ground, a hole, or beneath the grass.

"If you guys tell me what you have, I'll tell you what I have," said Billy.

"I thought you wanted to wait till we finish before we looked," said

Danny.

"I can hardly wait!" said Joey

"Me either! Let's hurry up look around a little more, then maybe trade," said Danny.

"Okay."

"Yeah. Let's do that."

The guys went back to their areas and picked up where they left off. Finally, after an hour had passed, Danny called to the others. They sat at the picnic table, spread their findings, and began their examination of what they found.

Joey started first.

"I found an old watch, a key chain, five or six pennies with old dates, and various other articles.

Billy found lots of things also but he felt his best find was a ring, a super ball, some marbles, and an artist paint brush.

Danny had found a hook with string attached, a belt buckle,

a compass, and an old motor from an old matchbox car. They traded, decided which things to keep and throw away. Soon, the time came for the others to go home.

"See you guys tomorrow!"

"Okay."

"See ya."

When Danny went inside, his mother saw that he had completed his treasure hunt.

"Is your junk hunt over?

"Treasures, Mom. Treasures."

"Oh really?" she smiled.

"Sure it is."

Just then, she dropped her spatula between the stove and the refrigerator.

"Oh no!" she exclaimed.

She tried to reach it, but with no such luck. The opening was too small for her hands to go through and the broom was too straight to grasp it, and the bottom of the broom was too wide for the opening.

"Danny!" she called.

"Yeah Mom?"

"I dropped my spatula between here," she pointed. "Do you think that you may be able to get it?"

Danny scratched his head in thought, then he suddenly began to smile.

"Wait just a minute, I'll be right back!"

He ran upstairs and rambled through his treasure box and came back with the hook and string he had found. His mother watched him lower it between the appliances. He quickly retrieved it and looked at his mother with a proud triumphant look.

"Why, thank you, son! Maybe it's not all junk after all!!"
"That's okay, Mom. It may be trash to you, but your trash is my treasure!!"

www.ingramcontent.com/pod-product-compliance
Lightning Source LLC
LaVergne TN
LVHW051923060526
838201LV00060B/4159